Leilah Jane King is a Bristol
her Iranian heritage. She gr
making light of family,
Her poetry is come
reflective sharing
of prejudic
and menta

Midnight Picnics in Tehran

Leilah Jane King

To Den
Here you go pal!
Hope you enjoy! Nice working with you!
Love from Leilah xx

Burning Eye

This edition published by Burning Eye Books 2019

www.burningeye.co.uk

@burningeyebooks

Burning Eye Books
15 West Hill, Portishead, BS20 6LG

ISBN 978-1-911570-66-0

Midnight Picnics in Tehran

to Mum and Dad, who have always been there for me.

CONTENTS

MIDNIGHT PICNICS IN TEHRAN

There are no seatbelts here.

Just imported techno that fills us with smiles and the night is
warm.
   The smell hums and radiates through your nostrils, petrol and
   dill; you are young

and you see your mum, she has sweat on the back of her neck
   and her hair is red.

The sweat is from talking and being here.

At this time of night everyone is awake. The entourage of cars
   meet in a disorderly way

but you find each other in the parks that are lit by lamplight and
   ice cream and pistachio.

Everyone is young, even the elders.

Your grandma is soft and always wearing tights, leading the
   discussion or silently watching and laughing with you
   wrapped between her legs.

Midnight picnics.

Salad, chicken and egg patties, saffron in rice and orange fizz,
   Zam Zam cola.

Your cousin is wearing cologne and there is so much in a smile.

Table tennis. The white pearl teeth and his brown eyes meet.In
the night there is a water fight and a football match and a real
   fight and tears and black tea with sugar cubes on tongues.

Midnight picnics in Tehran.

In the warm cloak, the respite of night. In the unkempt majestic living.

I see the sweat on the back of my mum's neck shining through her hair, from living.

BRIGHTON

Brighton, you bumbling bag of Bohemia!
You are sick from the wind, filled with gulls to die for and guys
    to take them.
You are Bram Stoker's approaching ascent. Tracing train lines to
    wealth, burning money with cockney tones.
You pot of pot-smoking crossdressing bus drivers, flamboyant
    feather-wearing diva-diving elopers.
You are brimming with an exorcism of wealthy slumming and a
    gabble of hard-luck windswept pill popping.

Brighton, you are sugar rush, you are experimentation,
    you are a butterfly at the coast silenced, its breath taken.
You are far from home. You are not provincial; you are manic,
    ecstatic and full-bodied in your extension.
You are the druid that levels fire-breathing nights. Skating
    children from Dogma who kill with hockey sticks.
You are Legends at 4am, false laughs, strangled homophobia,
    police tape on Upper Lewes. You are sordid and opaque.

Brighton, you are a shit-smelling hairdresser smothered in
    cologne.
You are an unwanted massage on the temples for
    near-expiration.
You are being thrown out of a house for 'Tory' leaning.
You are a dyke.
You are the real humdrum hatred your pretension can't hide.
You are powder. You are nearly walking home with men.
Brighton, you are.

TOCHAL MOUNTAIN

You walk alone;
your headscarf is pinned behind your ears.

With quick strides, hikers pass coffee shops and stray cats.

The side of the mountain is golden before the icy top,
a swimming pool of dust and jagged rocks.

You fall into colour, a catharsis of movement, serene
    endorphin.

When you take the first turn the headscarves are dropped.
This is a festival where the gangs of mountain dogs are men;
they are soft and if they bit you it would feel like being bitten
    by butter.

They howl occasionally and melt into the aridity.

The kaleidoscope of scarves litter the branches.

The colour cascades encasing the stripped trees,
a striptease down
to a type of modernity.
Unpeeling the prickled heat.

You do the same. Head down, eyes filled, you see her hair.

The root of a woman.

NIPPLES

I have a secret.
Two mounds of pale flesh that stretch across like a skyline taut
  and unwavering
but at the same time ageing and changing.
They live under my T-shirt and my shirt and jumper and I won't
  cage them.

Sometimes you can see,
when it's cold
especially...
breathing and rising, creeping and jibing.
Above the ribs, the mortal fishnet of bones and being.

And I hunch over sometimes to hide them
when I run. I run like Terminator's nemesis
from the sequel, hands out.
I will stab you through a milk carton.
The uncomfortable living pressing up on your eyes,
but most of the time

they're for tweaking and maybe feeding and I can see your dick,
  by the way.

HOUSE IN SHIRAZ

The afternoon was slow,
Iranian summer,
the sweat rolled down the collar like melon juice
they kept in the freezer.
They hid Dairy Milk in there too.
She let me have a block, but I was not to tell anyone.

I rested my stomach on the tiles like the stray cats;
the ceramic blue was
oceanic. The vents were filled with gnats,
so I slept at night
with a headscarf covering my face.
The light fabric prickled the skin and smelt like perfume.

The heat crept into the garden
and dried out the pond, shrinking the pomegranate tree,
made it more beautiful.
At the beginning, the starving tree is magnified. The tree's fruit,
    like eyes, are defined tightly,
its trunk is twisting, the tree's tautness reminds you of this
    perversity.

I watched the sun set slow, its cloak an apricot chador.
It was now cool enough for us to sit
outside and drink black tea.
We held a séance with the trays
and my cousin cried into the glass.
Among the skyline of throbbing mountains and dulling heat we
    played blackjack.
It gave us language to fill the hour.
Our eyes and their kindness were always enough.

PEEP SHOW

Wanking.
In a circle.
Steaming glass cubicle.
Two euros in a slot to have animation to look at.
Sultry teacher in explicit yoga turntable
rotisserie to remedy the lonely misogyny.
We snuck in together;
now that was romantic.
You holding my hand, while everyone else was wanking.

I CAN ONLY BE A WOMAN

I can only be a woman when I'm in Iran,
giving in to my delicacy, my secret femininity,
brittle shards that used to crack endlessly.

I used to cry a lot as a child and teen.
I don't know what I saw that frightened me, but I learnt to hide it,
becoming shrouded in the West; my tough side was best,
no loose-tongued, panel-clichéd, new-age feminist.

I'm better than that.

I'm a laddish lesbian pseudo-trans Braveheart
exacting my revenge on anyone who'll listen,
but brittle bones never change – they just gleam and glisten.

The material covers enforced by tyrannical mullahs felt just the
        same
as my new gender double-wrapping my curves in masculinity,
rebelling against second substandard citizenry.
Its latency is as potent as the overt discrimination we pity in the
        East.

But with prized patronising tones they paint their brides
as goddesses to be protected,
not demeaned, undervalued and rejected –
is it different or just the same?

Burdens, like burqas, are inanimate till we animate them
with meaning, suffering and shame-fulfilling prophecies –
some dogmatic, draconian, scripture-led hypocrisy to mobilise
        masses:
cherished like porcelain dolls under glass ceilings we are
        happiest.

I can only be a woman. If I love a man,
that's this grandiose visionary hetero plan – that we evade
        the truth,

avoid desires, pain that is as constant as throbbing veins
just to be the same – to lie like concrete statues with heavy
    panting.
Heavy stone limbs strewn over your body,
not exacting or exciting any part that matters,
but outward symmetry serves to flatter and fatten

the world with unwanting mothers and fathers.
People upon people – it's a hobby
that is foetal, mistreating, misguided, but its grandiose vision
of the hetero plan for me to love a man.

I can only be a woman when I'm in Iran.
Standing in Shiraz illuminated by the night,
the nocturnally lit life, the lamps tracing footsteps of lovers,
poets adorned by secret gardens to get lost in with another.
There's something comforting in their archaic crystallised
    notion of love.

Something which woos the woman in me, that softens the
    ferocity,

the misunderstandings.

I get lost in the oil-lit paths that trace like rivers around dead
    poets' tombs.

I get lost in myself, in the soft velvet of the night's hum,
    the wind
still warm, breathing on your neck

like your secret lover...

I left him there.

Our youth laid to rest. With Hafez the truth was written.
Inscribed in his stone, inscribed tonight, inscribed in his skin
    like this twisted pain.

if I could only be a woman again.

ALINA

We walked arm in arm to the Korean store;
our breath was cold, so visible to each other;
we made secret conversation;
you make this place seem more alive.

My hands were warm in yours, excited,
steps bouncing from the souls up.
I put my arm around you and inhaled.

We got to the store to collect supplies to shut ourselves in
and sat in one spot. I didn't want to leave to go to the toilet,
to switch the light on, suspended in an incomparable feeling
of contentment and excitement.

Your voice, your layers,
your simplicity, your truth,
your quiet complexities,
your modest giving of space, your forthrightness,
your teasing, your mystery, your gestures,
your withholding,
your holding me until the light leaves
and returns.

BACK

Your back is an imperfect arch,
a splintered muscle, delicate and fraught,
dislodged
in spasm from questions and agonising doubt.
It bends silently, absorbing the years.
You told me,
It's nice when someone has your back.
Love is like the implicit guardian
of a compost edge around a flowerbed.
It tells them, *Do not walk here,*
do not tread on the brightest colours,
the perfect petals we all have inside of us.

CORTISOL

I remember the big house and big cobwebs;
when I was younger memories always centred on a sultry
    summer
and the French windows that wouldn't lock.

Getting a bit older, the boys asked me to feel their arms
and I lived in a make-believe reality, let the hair on my legs
    grow long.

Shorts and white knees on the sofa kicked and picked it apart;
the dust fluttered along the light like dandelions in the wind.

I remember long walks and the smell of dogs,
notes on paper stuck to electric cars.
I remember always trying to make you laugh.
I remember having plenty of time to be tacky and oblivious,
watching films my dad had returned.

I remember expecting the same things you had, then seeing
    I was mistaken.
I realise now
this isn't a bad thing. It's just a thing.

TWENTY-SEVEN

You look ridiculous in heels,
like a child trying to drive a car.
It tightens the calves, you hear.

The houses around you fall like melting wax
from the speed at which you pass.
You are boring and bored. You are a first-world.
You have too much time.

The hairspray nauseates people in cars.
Obsession is a muzzle. It drowns the urine.
You mow down everyone.
It could be better than this.

SHIRAZ, IRAN

The city's sound trembles like tired muscle,
a crying stretch of morning prayer.

Speakerphones are perched on jeeps. They kick hot dust while
the steel-capped boots calm the atmosphere.

Your flight is tomorrow, you can't sleep combing artefacts,
you write your name on the back of a Polaroid.

In the dead of night, they fill the car. A rich voice
begins to sing. Your uncle explains the romantic words.

As you move along the road, there is a solitary chef
in a white apron selling kaleh pacheh to workers.

The sun falls on the jaw of the mountain;
spilling onto the roadside are men

with beautiful eyes.

KING

My mum called me princess. This was embarrassing.
I wanted to be a prince, in a way.

Wearing boys' school shoes and getting twigs in my hair.
Pissing standing up with my toddler brother, much to the
    disgust of my mother.

Trying to keep up with the men around me.
Enamoured by their secret vulnerability.
Following the adventure and cursed in a way.

Not tasting it fully. I can't fill these shoes. The trousers don't sit
    right.

I shared a love for the delicate, but what I admired in them,
my diluted replica I could not love.

The short hair carpet-like and stale, too much aftershave
or too much of what it was hiding, and
the brutal piggishness of misunderstanding.

Women: after an intermission, the finding, this painful
    discovery.
Every lesson awkwardly bore into your skin,
sticking like blood in your hair or food in your teeth.

I want to be a king, for me.
And I show my mum a princess, sometimes,
secretly.

THE PLACE WE LIVE

you're rusting like the tin he collects
the deaf guy in a string vest with the slow beep
defibrillating the football pitch
tracing the frayed white
up and down
it seemed bigger
when the joints and skin were thick and flexed
like cheese string and you lay in the lap
of your secret lover
you are
dazed and your eyes are dilated and scarlet
you wonder if she noticed
trying to recite Shakespeare, toes curling at the bottom of
    your skate shoes
backpack slumped down your backside
and she did the Lock Stock wash
spray, eye drops and chewing gum
scrunchies and white strapped
tops
the beginning of a chest or the end of beginning

MY BOTTOM BREAKFAST BITCH

You are my brunch bro, my designer dining partner, continental
    croissant cutch master.
I like having breakfast with no one else.
You are my morning wake-up wafer,
punch-pillow pancake crusader.
Sunrises without your suggestions for the best brunch
would be a shitstorm – an unfulfilled and bleak life.
I'd be stuck in bed with
soggy shit speared Shreddies and Saturday Kitchen
with that twat with the pink face and shirt.
I pay you back with
sonnets over ducks' eggs,
the yolk's sheen so vibrant
you cry a little bit.
Sometimes we play Scrabble and backgammon in
silence, overegging banter till someone gets upset...
or there is beautiful harmony, both triumphant with our
wordplay.
Horizons move in the autumn sunlight. We are free.
Until the mood changes,
a patter of rain through a broken sky.
A stranger's arm reaches across my face to the board.
'Ere, love, put that 'ere, you.
Silence.
*At first we humour him with Cheerio smiles and Coco Pops
    handshakes until I snap;*
with crackling fury I pop his tarty little face with pig spittle.

You weren't invited, dude.
Yes, you might be right – I have spelt wanka wrong
and it's not permissible even in the new Scrabble,
but I'd rather be defiantly ignorant
than share my breakfast time with you.
You have only got one
shot
lattes in this life
and consent is relevant even in a board game context.

Now fuck off.

THE GYM

You hear this is the new pick-up joint. Full face of makeup
before you mount the treadmill. We can't help looking at
    each other.

I am checking out your time.

Eyes bounce from the chest to the mirror to my chest to
    your chest
to my thighs to your thighs.

This place is weirdly hypnotic.

I like watching my calves bob in the drunk waves of rotating
    leather.
Sharpening the knife of my grunting self-perception.
Fuck yes, look at the legs on that.

A mirror one side and a window.
Here I am, world. Check out my ass.

THE OTHERS

They threw a milkshake out a travelling car by the pier south of
   Porthcawl

at the ginger in the band hoodie who pulled her sleeves down
   when she was nervous.

Luckily the shake was badly aimed and it only splattered her
   trainers a little bit.

It felt prejudiced and spiteful.

In some species the gingers are revered as the best kind,
   top dog,

more like tom cat. She wishes she was a cat sometimes

or just didn't live near Bridgend.

Some things are easier to arrange.

BERLIN

The city of must-see,
musky scents, damp denim, holey flesh, bad breath murals of
    Bowie, statues of Lenin, tears in socks.

A lot of effort to look like a little effort.

Hipster consorts gathered at our stop blaring Britpop, trailing
    the cult-smug noise in their wake.

I am a tremor, our jackets are now smoke jackets, trapped
    vacuum, sickly magnets.

Bottle of beer, best kebabs, worst morning, creatures of habit.

Bold ales, bold labels, at all times by all faces.

Suburbia graffiti, punk woman.

Vast and endless.

Come back in the summer.

CLUB ME TO DEATH

I am transfixed, statuesque, I do not know how to stand.
There are podiums in here for dancing and moving.
I find a nook, a corner to hunch over and load up on vagueness,
dehydrate for numb reprieve.

Why the fuck am I here?

Robot lady, rigid awkward gawker, freaky space molester.
Buzz killer, keep away, I might ask you about the weather.
There is a posture here, uninhibited gender.
I am an androgynous headbanger.
It just doesn't look right.

NO, I'M NOT TAKING THE FERRY

It all climaxed after months,
head in a gutter of stupor always scoping the corner,
and the night somehow led to her.

All that gory nonsense in two minutes of speaking; oh, wow,
    there's that feeling.
The anxiety snakes and ladders up from your groin to your heart
    to your stupid face.

I woke up at 7am, all fear and loathing, and rode my bike around
    the harbour.

This is my safeword. This is my first date. This is my postcard.

I decided I fell in love with the waitress.
After the coffee, I stood on the waterside where the level was
    a brink of blue.

I stood for what felt like an eternity watching the mild spring
    rain destroy the surface over and over again.

THE NUANCE AND PSYCHOLOGY OF LANGUAGE CAN SEEM QUITE ARBITRARY

The hotel smells of cannabis and aftershave.
I had seafood for dinner in a brown paper bag.
No paper plates. There was plastic cutlery and spaghetti on my
    chest.
I walked in the rain. The puddles doubted me
when I guessed my way there. Avoided the taxis,
resisting chat with the knowledge.
I laughed too much, forgot how to laugh,
danced for you in a smokescreen.
It's hard to relate.
You fill it with volume so it holds better.
Hold eye contact through a fish tank.
An angry Italian, built like a breadbin, barges you with his dense
    torso.
Everyone is used to pushing and bustling
and I feel vulnerable when you catch me
in the shoulder in a room
where there was enough space for it to not happen.
I am getting better at waiting for them to speak.
Silent in the box elevator when there is nothing to say.
The rain is drumming on the window.

MY UNCLE JAVAD

He showed me how to run around a track in a headscarf,
hair plastered to my forehead, dressed in black.

He was wearing an unashamed competitiveness
that was understandable.

He showed me how to move, how to meditate in a kinetic hustle.

No music, no thoughts. I see your eyes and your knowing smile.

MUSIC WITH YOU

You make it sentimental;
every soundtrack accompanies my quickstep. But it can really
    fuck with your motor skills.
Bumbling through the thick city air, stuttering through small talk.
I have the playlist you made me on repeat, melancholy, vaguely
    optimistic.
The song whimpers to an end;
the hope is all but extinguished, but you still flirt with the idea,
    you sad romantic.
You hid for an entire summer, told me I was hiding too, both
    pale under the moonlight.
Traipsing through Narroways. Listening, but I can't find you.

BELONG

It's strange to be sat so close to you. I can't look for long.
You are wearing a grey jumper, you smell the same and your eyes
   are fire.

You get up to leave, so I put my hand on your leg, gently push to
   tell you something I don't understand.

This confused desire is suddenly confronted in a new space that
   we do not share. I tell you and you smile.

We are together in our awkward bodies. You start jumping to
   rid yourself of it.

I follow you into the kitchen; I know you are going to leave. I do
   my best impression of someone who respects free will.

Arms holding onto arms onto arms. Bodies falling into flesh, into
   each other until it abruptly ends.

We share a goodbye kiss.
I belong to no one, I promise, not even you.

MY PRECIOUS

I go and sit on the stoop with you.
Soften the clink of the gate with a slow push, trying not to wake
the people in the house.

It's midnight, you should be inside. I push the chair out so when
I leave you can sit under the table, away from the rain and the
red reggae sky.

A boy shouts, *Tell her to sit*. I make myself passive while you
     gnaw.
He is too shy to stop and with masquerading aplomb bounces
away unnaturally into the darkness.

I sit and let you jump on me, pulling on the raggedy thread toy
with mastery until I get too tired and go home.

Tomorrow, my precioussss, I whisper, *I will walk you.*

WOMEN

One day you will leave me. I cannot fulfil a passage of legitimacy.
There are no well-versed vows, just a nagging doubt of inconsistent
hypocrisy.

I bear no fruit, only a pear shape.

Unobtrusive desire, soft expectations where we both know our
way around.

I cannot promise you an uncomplicated future or shield you from
your past.

I cannot put up a shelf for you or carry you over the threshold.

We settle for the occasional piggyback and I pretend that I am
tough.
I will feed the young lust and hedonism, calm the formative thrust
of twenty-somethings.

They told me it doesn't last, our love.

I will share your experience on the bus and intimidate the catcalls
with our long-held touch and laugh at their longing with secret
glances.

I will be your best friend, take you to the best talks and want
the same things. I will queue in the toilet with you and pass you
loo roll under the door. I will be on the same side of the picket line.
We will share everything, talk about fostering children.
Until one day, you're not there.

THE PLANT IS DEAD

She said she bought me the plant as it was hardy
and had little need of attention, as I was never around.
She wanted it to warm my new flat
but I wasn't sure where it should live.
In the sun or on the mantelpiece or hidden in the bedroom with
    our secrets.

Now you are not here to tell me where to put it.
I keep watering its dead body, waiting to throw it out.

NINE TREE SNOB

You lived on the corner above a barber,
a friendly guy who you mistook for a knob, when really he was
    just a dick.
Dick's barbers, Ricky, Scarface, who was being hustled by a rival
    hairdresser and the local kids;
they pointed out, You're too white to cut black hair,
and so the poor guy had to buy protection with free haircuts.

Anyway, we didn't like him at first till we saw the vulnerability,
so we did the right thing,
plus he stored a year's worth of your kitty litter in his back room.

Meanwhile you had plans
to move uptown, away from Dick and the kids in the street,
away from the disregard for recycling,
the blue house bust that got raided every week.
You found a place behind the sick shop
where they store the nurses and Bristol Uni students in Lego.

That's where you went, prophetically to the top
like the mechanics had planned it that way.
Obstacle cobbles, up a hill you could
only reach if you were young, brave
or you owned a car.

JAMAICA STREET

Property is theft. Nobody owns anything.
When you die, it all stays here.

Nobody owns anything
on Jamaica Street.
Saint Mungo
is in the hands of the empty.
Awkwardly present,
you pass the people pressing crutches on top of
stumbling blocks.
A pyramid
of steps to strain.

In the muggy heat,
I walk that way
as a shortcut,
turn my head to the ambulances,
bad decisions or
starting blocks
knocked out
like missing teeth.

No one owns anything,
apparently,
or shouldn't?

But the contrast in tenements
is present
and the mural shouts this
on the right side of the crescent
where there is time to be enlightened,
talk about gentrification.

Beyond the stabbings
in stairwells
we dance to African techno;
sneakers are swaying

from the phone lines;
you see them from the high rise
denoting death
misunderstood by the living,
ideologue art,
the melding of
misuse in men

The luxury of having a family to pick you up
when it all goes wrong.

ABOUT YOU

You are the in-between light,
you straddle day and night,
you make me drunk on lust
as we walk in each other's steps,
sleep where the other has slept,
carve out creases, fold our legs into laps.

You tell me I'm beautiful in this light.
I tell you no one has ever said that.
I say I'm scared of roads;
you ask if we should go this way instead.
You make me not want to sleep or eat again.

My house is a playground for midnight
picnics,
a nudist park for insomniacs.
I would kiss you through a jutting flick knife, through the blunt
    arbitrary slur
of a drive-by,
a car full of alleged humans
disturbed and howling
at two women kissing under the moonlight
under the half-cut night
above an allotment on a steep hillside.

CHRISTMAS SHAVINGS

performed as a song

It's that time, that time of year
to let your leg hair grow.
I wouldn't say to let oneself go
as that would be against my feminism.
Tonight
I shall take a peek at what I have grown,
my stubby legs,
oh, the mighty, oh, the brunette
burning buckwheat bonanza.
I strut around the house,
flashing children in the pantry
(we don't really have a pantry)
tonight,
so it must be
the end of
my fluffy freedom.
I look in the cabinet
for a razor,
one that isn't blunt or rusty.
That will do.
I shave myself with the blunt and rusty one, rusty one, yeah!

Yes, tonight
I light the candles.
I scream out to all my people, oh, my people,
I am ready today to unsheathe my stems, to make them shiny
    with shea butter taken from
my mother.
I start a countdown.
One, two...
Someone calls me, *Leilah!*
I get distracted.
I'd better blow out the candles.

Maybe I'll keep them.
My bushy babies,
calves and ankles, quads and bum holes;
yes, bum holes will forever be.
I'm not going to shave if you ask me to, no,
shave if you ask me to, no.
Fuck the patriarchy, fuck the patriarchy
fuck you, Mr Patriarchy,
fuck the patri', fuck fuck the patri',
fuck you,
Dad.

HEART-SHAPED HAIR

Heart-shaped
hair
grown for two years.
She says,
Don't cut it;
it smells clean and that's enough.
No, It's a trap.
The East knew what women's hair could do.
You need to bottle it up,
tame the masses from their garbled grasps of desperation,
black and blue on the eyes
and cold in being held,
I felt.
It doesn't matter.
I see you;
you're like a proud animal,
an aloof feline
skirting my calf, disappearing,
but always beautiful.

PLATFORM NUMBER 7

You'll find us,
two women stooped at the station
in the dirt with the pigeons.
We sat down slow against the furthest pillar,
all knees in light blue jeans
and pale shadows.

I was hiding your mouth
to the world, eyes peeping.
The seagull stole
the sandwich right out of your hand
and I felt embarrassed watching you swear at it.
I guess it meant something,
the abruptness,
trying to talk heavy with no privacy,
the tannoy rupturing our train
of thought.

EAST

East, let's go.
Pack your bag, bring sandwiches and your best dress, meet me
    outside Tesco.
I'm trying to charm you with half-smiles, let you see I'm all fear.
We cycle now it's half past spring, summer's creeping in.
My lips are forever dry and you are lip balm forever.

East, let's go.
I will hold out until arrival, let you meditate and get me drunk
even if tomorrow is deathly.
I'll loosen the anxiety for one night with you. There is nothing
but heart of hormone, ill for impulse.
There is nothing paralleled to this; the neck, the spine, the eyes
    are hidden. Not now; let's go. The rain is coming.

YOGA

I am imagining you in a gymnasium-type hall, maybe at the top
  of Gloucester Road.
They're playing Bonobo and you are on the far left
wearing black Adidas and a top that makes me jealous
that anyone has visual access.
You are rosy-cheeked and the endorphins make your eyes deep
  and more blue
I miss the sound of you.
I imagine you stretching and holding in a way I have never done,
nor could I tell you how this would actually look.
The mats are rolled and you are one of the last to leave,
talking with your friend and walking home under the amber;
the evening only shines from the nape of your neck.

DADS IN THE PARK

My dad is tall,
formidable, not a ball boy but a ball boy sometimes for me.
Once a winger in a rugby team. He smiles out from under a
     scrum of entangled bandaged knees.
My dad shouts the loudest and makes others experience severe
     cowardice
He is always prepared, apples and chairs. He brings an umbrella
and wears joggers and a beige jacket, a woolly hat so worn it's
     lost its elastic;
it's drooping but it still works, he thinks, I think.

He puts my frozen blue hands under his arms to warm them and
     speaks deeply.
My dad is the tall guy on the sideline shouting, probably making
     the other dads feel quiet or meek,
but not me. He makes me feel like I'm kind of a big deal
     on Sundays, at least.

A PERSIAN JEWEL

When regarding the female form that dwells
in the Middle East, their form that shines,
her brightest silver casts its sensory spells,
the deepest brown orbs of warm surprise,
these eyes that burn into your own
and make one's skin much paler than once known,
whose elastic curls of darkened knots
ensnare the faithful to doubt the stone
that bound their love that's now forgot
and left them torn and all alone.

For that divine creature that inspires love
misleads mere mortals with a blistering smile
and the admirers regard the enchanted dove
that this eastern jewel has conjured
for the shortest while.

ACKNOWLEDGEMENTS

Thanks to Bridget Hart and Clive Birnie for releasing my first book and giving me a platform to perform; to Lydia Beardmore, Carly Etherington and Tom Sastry for helping me edit; to Andi Langford Woods and the Halo crew for nurturing my passion, to Jeremy Toombs and the Art House poetry community for many inspiring nights; to Chester Giles for our poem exchanges, to the alternative feminist music and poetry scene in Bristol notably Lisa Rose and the Honey Art Show; to my football team for helping me kick things on days off from writing.

Lightning Source UK Ltd.
Milton Keynes UK
UKHW041350020719
345424UK00001B/66/P